WRITER AND ILLUSTRATOR:
SHIRLEY WILLIS was born in Glasgow. She has worked as an illustrator, designer and editor, mainly on books for children.

READING CONSULTANT:
BETTY ROOT was the Director of the Reading and Language Information Centre at the University of Reading for over twenty years. She has worked on numerous children's books, both fiction and non-fiction.

TECHNICAL CONSULTANT:
PETER LAFFERTY is a former secondary school science teacher. Since 1985 he has been a full-time author of science and technology books for children and family audiences. He has edited and contributed to many scientific encyclopaedias and dictionaries.

EDITOR:
KAREN BARKER SMITH

Published in Great Britain in MMXIX by
Book House, an imprint of
The Salariya Book Company Ltd
25 Marlborough Place, Brighton BN1 1UB
www.salariya.com

ISBN: 978-1-904642-62-6

SCRIBO   BOOK HOUSE   SCRIBBLERS

1 3 5 7 9 8 6 4 2

A CIP catalogue record for this book is available from the British Library.

Printed and bound in Malaysia.

Visit
www.salariya.com
for our online catalogue and
free fun stuff.

PAPER FROM
SUSTAINABLE
FORESTS

WhiZ Kids

CONTENTS

Wherever you see this sign, ask an adult to help you.

WhiZ Kids
Tell me how far it is

Written and illustrated by

SHIRLEY WILLIS

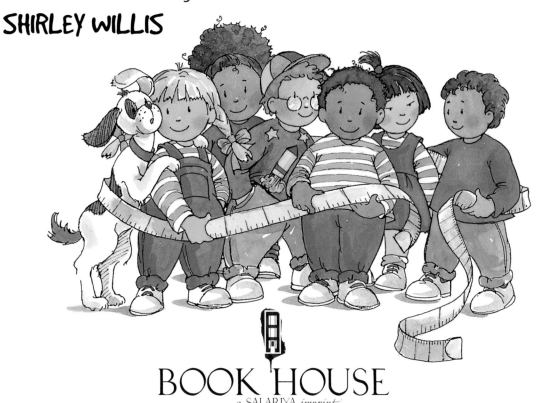

BOOK HOUSE
a SALARIYA *imprint*

WHAT IS DISTANCE?

The space between things is called distance.

Some distances are very small.

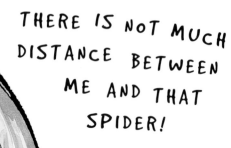

THERE IS NOT MUCH DISTANCE BETWEEN ME AND THAT SPIDER!

Some distances are very big. The Moon is far away from the Earth.

Distance can be any size.

WHICH WAY IS IT?

Distance can be measured in any direction – up or down, left or right.

The swimming pool is long in one direction and wide in the other.

LENGTH

WIDTH

I CAN SWIM ACROSS THE POOL BUT NOT TO THE OTHER END... IT'S TOO FAR!

CAN YOU GUESS DISTANCE?

You need to know the distance from your home to your school so that you can get there on time.

You can't measure every distance – you have to guess how far it is.

I'VE THROWN THAT BEAN BAG A BIT TOO FAR!

IS IT NEAR OR FAR?

You will need: • Two bean bags

1. Place a bean bag at your feet as a marker. Throw the other one.
2. Measure the distance between the bean bags in steps.
3. Throw the bean bag again. This time guess if it has gone further before you measure the distance in steps. Is your guess right?

Try guessing distances as you walk. Guess how many steps it will take to reach the next lamppost or the end of the road.

HOW FAR IS IT?

The distance between places is longer when a road is hilly or winding.

WHICH PIECE OF STRING IS LONGER?

Both pieces of string are the same length. One piece looks shorter because it twists and turns. A road that twists and turns will be longer than a straight road.

IS IT THE SAME DISTANCE?

The distance between each house is the same. It doesn't take long to go from the first house to the second house: the road is straight and flat. It takes much longer to get to the third house because the road is longer – it goes up and over the hill.

CAN YOU MEASURE DISTANCE?

Before there were rulers, people used their bodies to measure distance.

They measured short distances by thumb-widths or handspans.

HANDY MEASURES

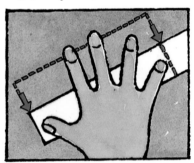

Stretch your hand out wide. The distance from your thumb to your smallest finger is called your handspan.
(Mark your handspan width on a strip of paper. You can now use it to measure.)

Measure this page with your thumb. How many thumb-widths is it?

What else can you find to measure in thumb-widths or handspans?

Measure across pages 14 to 15 in handspans.

People measured longer distances by the length of their foot, arm or stride.

How many handspans tall are you?
Ask a friend to hold their hand on a wall to mark your height. Now measure your height in handspans from the floor up to their hand.

THIS DISTANCE IS CALLED AN ARM-SPAN!

HOW DO WE MEASURE CORRECTLY?

GROWN-UPS' ARMS ARE MUCH LONGER THAN MINE!

Using the body to measure anything creates problems. People are all different sizes, so their answers are different, too.

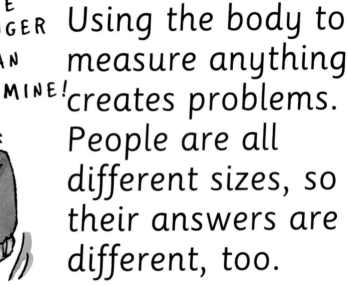

Hands are all different shapes and sizes – so are feet.

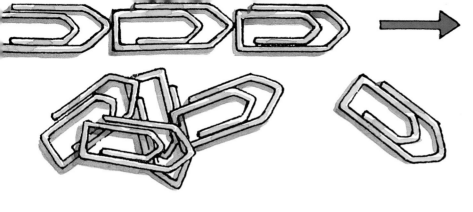

Measure this page in thumb-widths – is everyone's answer the same? Now measure it with paperclips laid end to end.
This measurement is the same every time because the paper clips don't change size.

If everyone used the same 'lengths' to measure with, they'd get the same result.

STRAWS ARE GOOD FOR MEASURING TOO!

17

WHAT IS A METRE?

In 1791, scientists in France worked out a measurement of length for everyone to use. It was called the metre.

This is the metric system that we use today.

100 CENTIMETRES = 1 METRE
1000 METRES = 1 KILOMETRE

LET'S MEASURE

Put your thumb or small finger at the bottom of this ruler (right). Ask your classmates to do the same. Find out who has the biggest handspan in your class. Who has the smallest?

A metre is divided into 100 equal parts. Each part is called a centimetre. 1000 metres is called a kilometre.

CENTIMETRES

19
18
17
16
15
14
13
12
11
10
9
8
7
6
5
4
3
2
1

WHICH DISTANCE?

We measure short distances in centimetres (cm).

We measure longer distances in metres (m).

CM IS SHORT FOR CENTIMETRES!

M IS SHORT FOR METRE!

KM IS SHORT FOR KILOMETRE!

We measure
very long distances
in kilometres (km).

MY SCHOOL IS
1 KM AWAY BUT...
THE SUN IS ABOUT
150 MILLION
KM AWAY

LET'S MEASURE

How big is this book –
would you measure it in
centimetres, metres or
kilometres?

How wide is it across pages
20 to 21?

How high is page 21?

Measure things around
you. Try to choose
the right kind of
measurement each time.

WHY DO WE NEED TO MEASURE DISTANCE?

If shoes are too small, they hurt our feet.

HOW BIG ARE YOUR FEET?

You will need:
- A sheet of paper
- Felt-tip pen
- Ruler

1. Take off your shoes.
2. Put one foot on the paper and draw around it.
3. Now do the other foot.

Are both feet the same length?
Measure them and see.
Ask your friends to measure their feet too.
Whose feet are biggest?
Whose feet are smallest?

ONE FOOT
MAY BE
BIGGER THAN
THE OTHER!

We measure things
for many reasons.

If a bridge isn't
long enough,
you can't cross
to the other side.

Furniture has to
be the right height
to be useful
and comfortable.

THIS CHAIR IS
TOO LOW!

WHY DO WE MEASURE OURSELVES?

We measure ourselves so that clothes and shoes fit when we buy them.

We measure the height of babies and children to see if they are healthy and growing well.

THIS ISN'T MY SIZE!

MAKE A HEIGHT CHART

You will need:

- A piece of wallpaper, 1.5 metres long
- Felt-tip pen
- Measuring tape
- Drawing pins
- Stick-on labels

1. Pin the paper to the wall - this is your chart.
2. Get help to mark your height clearly on it.
3. Carefully measure and record your height beside the mark. (Measure from the floor up.)
4. Write your name and height on a label. Stick it to the chart beside your height mark.

Measure your classmates too.
Who is the tallest in your class?
Who is the smallest in your class?

You grow a little taller each year until you are about 20 years old. Some children grow faster than others.

CAN ROUND THINGS BE MEASURED?

The measurements of a round object have special names: the circumference, the diameter and the radius.

CIRCUMFERENCE

DIAMETER

RADIUS

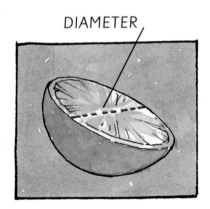

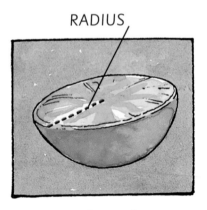

Measure all the way around an orange.
This is the circumference.

Take half an orange.
Measure across the middle.
This is the diameter.

Measure from the centre to the edge.
This is the radius.

The distance around
a round object is called
the circumference.

The distance across
a round object is called
the diameter.

THE DISTANCE AROUND
THE EARTH IS ABOUT
40,075 KM

The distance from the
middle to the edge
of a round object
is called the radius.

HOW FAR AWAY IS THE MOON?

The Moon is far away. It is about 384,400 km away from the Earth.

This distance is so big that it takes a spacecraft 3 days and nights to reach the Moon.

ZOOM!

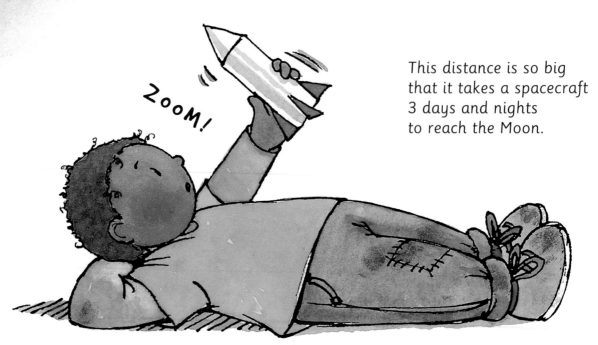

Imagine going around the world nine or ten times without stopping. That distance is like going to the Moon.

DID YOU KNOW?

A giraffe's neck can be 2 m long.

Blue whales are the biggest animals on Earth. They can be as long as 30 m.

The tallest living thing in the world is a tree in California (115.5 m tall).

The highest mountain in the world is Mount Everest (8848 m high).

A flea is tiny, but it can jump 600 times its own body length.

THAT FLEA CAN JUMP A LONG WAY!

GLOSSARY

arm-span	The distance measured by the length of an arm.
centimetre (cm)	A unit of length measuring one hundredth of a metre.
circumference	The distance measured around a circle.
depth	The distance measured from the top down to the bottom.
diameter	The distance across the centre of a circle. It is measured in a straight line from one side to the other.
distance	The amount of space between two points or objects.
hand-span	The distance measured between the tips of the thumb and little finger when stretched apart.
height	The distance measured from the bottom up to the top.
kilometre (km)	A unit of length that measures 1,000 metres.
length	The distance measured from one end to the other.
metre (m)	A unit of length that measures 100 centimetres.
metric system	A system of measurements that is based on a metre length.
radius	The distance measured in a straight line from the centre of a circle to the circumference.
thumb-width	The distance measured by the width of a thumb.
width	The distance measured from one side to the other.

INDEX